Roger,

May God Bless you
and your family.
Do Great Things!

The Mortgage Millionaire

Sales and Life Strategies That Can Take You to The Next Level

William B. Bronson

authorHOUSE®

AuthorHouse™
1663 Liberty Drive, Suite 200
Bloomington, IN 47403
www.authorhouse.com
Phone: 1-800-839-8640

First published by AuthorHouse 5/6/2008

ISBN: 978-1-4343-7267-3 (sc)

Printed in the United States of America
Bloomington, Indiana

This book is printed on acid-free paper.

Dedication

This book is dedicated to my children. I hope I can instill in them some wisdom that I gained from difficult lessons in my life. At least I can try to give them some insight, which may help them learn from situations in their own lives. Without my children, I may have had an entirely different perspective on goal setting and may have lacked the motivation to succeed at all costs. I thank them for loving me and being there for me to love.

A wise man once told me that it is doubtful our children can be given the wisdom that we have gleaned from working long hours, dealing with people and situations we cannot control, and making mistakes. For wisdom, they will have to do the same, unfortunately.

Perhaps, I can help them along this road.

I would also like to thank my wife, Christie, without whom the object of my dedication would not have been possible. She is the most incredible partner and soul mate I could have asked for. She is the cement, which binds our family together.

"It's true you cannot fail if you don't try, but neither can you succeed."

TABLE OF CONTENTS

FOREWORD

By Todd Avery

When Bill asked me to write the foreword for his book, I was a little bit nervous, to tell you the truth. First of all, I've never before been asked to write a foreword for a book. Secondly, when a friend and colleague, who respects your opinion and trusts your honesty, asks you to, not only review but also, write, what is essentially the introduction to his first book, that's double the pressure! What if it stinks? What if I stink? What if it doesn't make sense and I have to be the one to break it to him? Funny how our minds work, isn't it?

Well, after just finishing the rough draft, I can tell you that, among other things, I am excited. I'm excited in a way that I'm not sure I've ever really been before. I'm excited with a quiet confidence that is both bold and humble, like the author himself. As I sit here at one o'clock in the morning, I'm almost overwhelmed with energy, ideas, and belief, all at once. Energy, ideas, and belief that I already had inside of me, that came back to life again as I spent my last two evenings clinging to every word, and every "Billism," found inside this cover. Having been in sales of some type, from Amway to home mortgages, for over twenty years, and consequently having read almost every self-help and PMA book out there, I never know when I'm going to run across the next book that truly has a life changing impact on me. I can now say, without a doubt, that my good friend, "Texas," as I call him, has put together a book that did just that! The wisdom and truth about, not only the mortgage industry but, all sales careers, that Bill shares, as only a big-hearted Texan like him can share, is priceless. Congratulations on a great job Bill, and thank you for "telling it like it is," in a short and sweet way, that can truly help sales people understand the basics that are most important. Your knowledge, which you so passionately shared in this book, is both timeless and precious and I am grateful you offered me the chance to read it first! Your heart and soul are in the pages of this book, and they poured out as I read it. If that was still your mission, as we discussed some time ago, then all I have to say is "mission accomplished!"

For those of you about to read this book, whether you are new to the sales industry and trying to figure out how to get started, or a seasoned veteran who is always searching to fuel that passion for what we do, you will, no doubt, find what you are looking for, as I have, in the pages of this book. Bill's method of delivery, through conversation, is so powerful that I don't think the true message of it all would have come across in any other way. Beware of only one thing as you begin reading. Make sure that you have enough time to finish it before you start!

May God Bless you all!

Todd Avery
Former COO, Carteret Mortgage Corporation

FOREWORD

By Sifu Lance Fleming

This book, "The Mortgage Millionaire," should be placed in more than one section of a bookstore or library. It's a culmination of career-relevant, "how to" information, ethical business practices, self motivation, inspiration, and family values.

In lieu of attempting to expound on the specific contents of the book and its multiple facets, I will tell you more about the author and his background that is behind all that is within these pages.

I have known Bill since my sophomore year in high school over twenty years ago, and have had the opportunity to witness his struggles and achievements. The advice and inspiration that he shares comes from tough experiences, discipline, and wisdom that can only be gained through perseverance.

The things that brought difficulties and hardships for Bill, early in his career, are the character traits that serve him so well in his success today. For example, he refused to "sell out" or to "buy in" to anything that didn't match up to his ethics and principles.

Bill was always, and still is, an "out-of-the-box" thinker. This quality, coupled with a genuine care for people and an attitude for serving his community, has made him a mentor in his business and personal life.

Upon entering the mortgage business, he was presented with a typical desk, phone, mediocre leads system, and a mandatory quota. When he inquired about the best way to develop business, he was instructed to start calling leads. In the industry, this is known as "the trenches," and Bill spent a great deal of time there.

From the very beginning, he began rewriting and reshaping the dynamics of finance, resulting in a more honest and efficient service for the community. Not many at his place of business appreciated his quest for change, nor did he appreciate their attitudes about customer service. For Bill, this was not a deterrent; but it actually fueled his resolve for making big changes in the way business was conducted. Through hard work, he received many awards and realized that his higher calling was still not fulfilled. So, in 2001 he broke away from retail mortgage lending and opened a brokerage office. Since then, he has continued to bloom as a mentor and teacher to those who share a similar passion for helping people. At the same time, he has maintained a relentless passion for learning.

Bill has been a student of Hurricane Combat Arts, under my direction, since 2003. His desire to learn the Hurricane system was not done to achieve rank or status. This endeavor was to help protect his family and others who couldn't protect themselves. This, I've learned, is in his nature.

It's an odd experience to see a person who has taught me so much, and whom I hold in such high esteem, be so humble about learning new things. It truly demonstrates his appreciation for knowledge and understanding, as well as his strength of character. He often says, "Every man is my teacher," and I know that it's not an empty phrase. I have learned much about teaching and learning through my professional and personal life with Bill. We regularly discuss our professions and, as we seek to better ourselves, I learn a great deal about teaching and learning. He is a boundless source of insight and encouragement for me, and it's an honor to call him a friend and brother.

As you read this book, you will undoubtedly see into the character that fuels him to achieve greater things. He openly shares with you strategies and encouragement for succeeding in business and in life. He shares this because he truly believes in humanity, morality, and the potential for achievement in everyone.

Bill is a great friend, mentor, student, and teacher, with a strong commitment to God, family, and community. I believe you will both enjoy and benefit from what he shares in the following pages.

Thank you, Bill, for honoring me with the privilege of sharing my thoughts of you and your book. There are not enough words to begin to say it all.

Fraternally and Sincerely,

Lance A. Fleming
President – World Combat Martial Artists Association
Sifu "Teacher" – Hurricane Combat Arts Academy of Texas

INTRODUCTION

This book is designed to help everyone who reads it, not just mortgage professionals or salespeople. "Sales" is for life and all of us need to learn how to better present our ideas, products, and services to any audience. Whether you're trying to get your point across to a colleague or interview for a job, some of the lessons covered in this book can help.

We all need some experienced advice in different areas of our lives. I've spent the better part of my life learning from experiences most people would consider failures. But, I realized something that others seem to have forgotten. A failure is what you make from it. Have you ever heard, "When life gives you lemons, make lemonade"? When you have a failure, learn from it. Taking a failure and making it an educational experience is easy if you understand that your success is obtained by using the collection of lessons that you learned from those failures, and turning them into a plan of action. None of us are good at anything without practice and work. Practice gives you experience; experience includes a great deal of failures. Don't let them hinder your drive and motivation to succeed. Let them fuel it!

My sincere hope is that, after reading this book, you will have better clarity about certain situations that you may now find difficult, and that you will also have the straight advice about how to better deal with people in your professional and personal life. Lastly, I hope that you will have a renewed motivation, and the tools, to achieve success.

Become who you wish to become before the materialization of it catches up to you. Be who you wish to become. I know it's difficult to understand, but with some thought, you'll get it. Don't just strive to become better than you are today. Be better, tomorrow, than you are today.

"Do or do not, there is no try"
YODA

"You can only realize true career satisfaction when your total efforts not only benefit each other, but also you and every potential client, who comes to you for help."
Me

THE BEGINNING

(As I sit in the waiting room of my ghostwriter's office, I can't help but feel a little apprehensive. After all, I train people for a living, speak in front of groups, and never seem to have a problem expressing my thoughts. Years of advice are gathered in my head covering countless topics. So why am I about to allow someone else to write my book? I've started numerous times to gather it all up and write "The greatest sales advice ever written," or other catchy possible book titles. It seems to be more fun to think up titles and ideas than to actually complete the work. This writer, Amelia, came highly recommended by several publishers and authors. But, who is she that I am not? Pondering this thought, I look out, through ceiling-to-floor thick glass windows, into the landscaped courtyard of this southwestern styled two-story office building. It has a nice courtyard garden area with redwood benches under the shade of veteran maple trees that are in the process of turning colors of gold and red. It seems like a nice place to sit and think, but nobody's there. I'd rather be out there than in here. My mind starts to wander. I think of what questions Amelia will ask, if she can probe my thoughts deep enough to get the information needed for a quality piece of work, and if she's a good enough writer to satisfy my taste. Why am I here? No more time to wonder, the door is opening.)

Amelia?

Yes, how are you? Please come in Mr. Bronson.

You may call me Bill.

(She's dressed professionally, and looks smart, in a nice gray wool suit with her hair up. She looks like the person my mind had conceived from our telephone conversation, except she's a little older. Her voice, with a light melodic Irish accent, had me picturing someone much younger. This lady looks ready for business as we sit down and she reaches for her voice recorder.)

Did you bring the outline and other materials we talked about?

I did.

(I hand her a thick stack of notes, drawings, and emails. She looks surprised at the mass of it all.

She takes some time to browse through my writings. Then, she remarks that they look well written and wonders why I need her.)

(I'm usually very thoughtful, but I blurt out,)

I don't know. Maybe I don't.

(Then recovering a little)

My brain can't seem to focus on writing it in any intelligible format. There's too much. Maybe I'm just lazy.

(There's a silence. She doesn't look happy with my answer and I wonder if maybe I offended her. Writing is serious business and maybe I insulted the craft. Oh well, what do I care. I'm here, intending to spend a great deal of money for her to do it.)

Okay, you seem to have a tremendous amount of different ideas to get across. So, let's not dilly dally around and get to it. I'd like to start with your outline since it's your own created format. Then I'll see what improvements I can make.

What I want you to do is to relax and put your feet up. Just think of nothing for a moment.

(I do as she requests and sink down into a large, very comfortable, brown leather chair. It's worn and looks as if hundreds of people have found comfort in it. It's perfect for relaxing and allows my mind to open up. If nothing else, maybe I'll buy one just like it for my office.)

Okay, what we're going to do is this. I'll ask you open-ended questions, for the most part, and you answer as clearly, thoughtfully, and as detailed as you can. Ready?

Yes, let's get to it.

Tell me about who you are in your profession.

I'm a trainer, mentor and recruiter in the mortgage business. My mission is to equip mortgage loan officers with the knowledge and good advice that can help them succeed past their expectations. However, my purpose runs much deeper than my vocation. By that, I mean that I have a drive, which stems from a spiritual relationship much larger than my own aspirations, to empower others and to help them.

Technically, I'm a vice president for one of the largest mortgage brokerages in the country, Founder of JobsForLoanOfficers.com, and an agent for a company that helps home and business owners pay off their mortgages in record time. Mainly, I'm a team builder and motivator.

MINDSET

Mindset is the first topic in your outline. Do you feel it is the most important?

Yes, I definitely do. Without the proper mindset, you can struggle for years, even with good motivation and other positive attributes, and not reach your potential.

Tell me about mindset as it relates to the mortgage business.

The power of your mind is an incredible thing. Mindset is the first thing to master going into any endeavor. Actually, you don't need to master it before you get started, you just need a good handle on it; mastery could take a lifetime. A good mindset keeps loan officers from falling into bad habits that can kill potential sales. A bad mindset can keep them from approaching people the right way, and it contributes to discontentment about their performance. It's important to approach this business from a position of power. Because we find funding, potentially hundreds of thousands of dollars for a client, we should feel like a bank president on the road. A bank president actively promotes the bank and its services. We should think of ourselves as the leader of our own businesses.

Loan officers should take charge of their careers and develop a sense of ownership and urgency.

You sound like you love to teach. Would it help you explain things easier if you thought about this interview as a training class for me?

It may.

Okay, tell me more about mindset. Act like I'm a loan officer and you're teaching me directly.

Okay.

You know, writing this book, if I could convey just one extremely valuable piece of advice, it's this: no matter what the situation is in sales, it's all in your head.

What I mean by this is…If you think something is a big deal you will spread that thought to others. If you think the market is slow and people won't buy from you, it doesn't matter if it's just a little slow, people will not only believe it, but will also spread it around. They can smell apprehension on you. If, however, the economy is a little slow and you're convinced it's just a normal cycle, and nothing to worry about, this will rub off also. People look into other people's eyes to find fear, apprehension, worry, stress, and other telltale signs of trouble. It's called body language and it encompasses a ton of things.

What kind of things?

Things like speech rate, tone, and quiver in your voice; shifty eyes, posture, gate, stride, gestures, and other mannerisms can give people a window to your innermost thoughts. Mastering this can increase your power in sales, and in life, dramatically.

Is that what you wanted?

Exactly! Go on.

I saw a good friend of mine not long ago. He said, "Hey, I'm sure upset I didn't take you up on that refinance. The rates have gone through the roof, haven't they?" He didn't ask me about it. He told me about it.

I looked puzzled and then said, "What are you talking about? They're lower than when we talked three weeks ago!"

When I asked him where he got that helpful little tidbit of news, he said he heard it on the television. Well that's a surprise!

TV news can be good and educational. But, it can also be the single most destructive news medium in our society. Sometimes they "fly off half cocked," as my dad says, stretching the truth and causing panic. Most of the time, they seem to focus on the negative. Things on TV spread like wildfire and, if the information is bad or misrepresented, it can cause all kinds of trouble. It's basic human nature to pay attention to things that could be dangerous, so fear sells. I'm right and here's proof. Some years back, a feel good news program failed due to poor ratings. They only focused on things that made people feel good, things people did for others, and other good will stories. But, the program failed because it didn't have enough "dirt" in it, hurting its ratings. People like a good scandal, but it can be a dangerous combination when you get your facts from it. Here's a truth most people don't grasp.

Do you realize that if we went into a recession and the news didn't pound it to death like they do, people would keep doing things as usual, buying and selling like normal, and the recession could be, potentially, extremely mild? People wouldn't lose their jobs or go out of business, stock prices wouldn't plummet, and many other things would be avoided. It would be an unrealized loss because the scare wouldn't have been acted upon.

Were you a loan officer during a recession?

A slight one, yes, but I don't' dwell on negatives and I don't act on scare tactics. I try to always spread optimism and downplay negativity.

I surpassed most loan officers in the country when I had to sell a 9% rate to a borrower with a 700+ credit score and charge ten discount points just to get them a rate that low. That wasn't exactly the best time in mortgage lending history. But, I won awards at a time when most loan officers were quitting the business altogether. I never let rate and other fluctuations affect me because they're all relative to the market and don't truly affect business flow. Houses are still being built, bought, sold, and refinanced. People are still using available equity to pay off high interest credit card debt. Business is conducted under any market condition, and let me teach you a little more truth here. When the news says rates are going up or down, they're talking about short term rates. This impacts credit cards, credit lines, auto loans and the like. This doesn't affect mortgage rates the way you might think. Long-term bond rates, "Mortgage Backed Securities" or "Mortgage Bonds," are more effective in predicting mortgage rates, not the 10-year Treasury note. While the 10-year T-Note sometimes heads in the same direction as Mortgage Bonds, it's not unusual to see them move in opposite directions. The news is not usually a good source for what's to be expected when you apply for a mortgage loan. Most loan officers don't realize this either. In general, as far as the news is concerned, you should double check with several other sources on any given subject, before you spread it to others and certainly, before you act on it.

Why would I, as a loan officer, need to know about this?

Because you need to know it so you can teach your clients. My point is this: don't let the news you read or hear unreasonably change your actions or those of your client's. Tell them what I just told you. Preach it because it's true.

How you feel about a controversial subject will rub off on your clients. High rates, too many points, taking too long to close, ARM versus fixed, etc. You must sell yourself before you can sell anyone else. By this, I mean you must believe it before you preach it. You must also genuinely have something good to offer in order for you to believe in it. If you have a good product or service, don't be afraid to tell your clients about it. Brag a little about what you have to offer. I always start with some exciting or happy news before I tell my clients something tough. For instance, I would tell my client they're approved and we can save them over $200 per month before I tell them the rates went up a little. Because the rate going up didn't hurt my ability to help them, I don't mind it being the last thing I mention. The next time you think, "They'll never go for that," think again. It's all in your head. They will follow.

Sounds like good advice. Preach what I believe and believe what I preach.

Exactly! Never spread news rumors or scare tactics. Even if we're really heading into a recession, no good will come from panic. Even if mortgage rates are really going up, there's no good reason for halting the normal flow of business. Rates are only what you pay if you make every payment on time for the whole term of the loan. A short time of high rates isn't going to affect you that much, especially on a payoff acceleration plan like the one I offer.

APPEARANCES

Okay, moving right along on your outline, tell me about appearances. Is this about what to wear or speaking in front of people?

What to wear.

Okay, what should you wear and why. Just tell me everything you want to about the topic of dress.

Okay, first of all, let me ask you a question. Should I, as a man, wear a coat and tie when meeting with clients?

Yes, I should think.

You're partially right, but mostly wrong.

Why mostly wrong?

Make no mistake, a properly tailored suit is great, but it may send the wrong message. I believe that, many times, wearing a suit without a tie is best; nice pants and a blazer with a crisp button down oxford may also be good. A suit and tie are intimidating to many people unless you're in a corporate environment, and even then there are instances where losing the tie may be best.

For you, and other women, I think it's easier because you have a natural sense of fashion. But, stay classy, as you look today, and don't be afraid to let your hair down. Just leave the jeans at home. There's no reason to meet clients in a pair of jeans unless you feel it's appropriate, as in farm or ranch situations.

So why should men lose the tie?

I'm not saying to lose the tie always, but it's not a given necessity. I'm not the kind of person who would wear one just to avoid standing out.

Let's discuss that for a moment. If you were a male loan officer I'd tell you like this:

If you're the only one in the room without a tie, who says that's a bad thing? After all, you're the one in charge of the meeting, right? A crisp white or blue shirt and a charcoal pinstripe suit may look pretty hip. You're confident enough with yourself to pull it off, right?

Wearing a tie just to fit in with everyone around you may just be a sign of insecurity and a social need to be accepted. You're not there to fit in or be accepted as one of the sheep. You're there to be accepted and respected as someone who has world class service to offer and is the best at what you do. Look at what the boss normally wears. Not the old white shirt and tie, usually. The boss dresses a bit more comfortably or flashy, depending on the boss. I've walked into a company full of cookie-cutter suits, plain blouses and blazers, past the drab cubicles and fluorescent lighting, to a radically different setting. The boss's office had actual light bulbs in lamps, paintings on the wall, and he was dressed in a golf shirt with khaki pants. I'm not saying a tie is not sometimes appropriate. I would just caution you to use your good judgment and question your motives.

"He who seeks the approval of man will undoubtedly be disappointed."

Nice quote. Who said it?

Me, I think. I've come up with tons of them.

What about the saying, "when in Rome do as the Romans do?"

Now, I know I didn't come up with that one!

That's not what I meant. Can you comment on it?

I think that it's misinterpreted much of the time. I say, when in Rome conform to the laws and customs there, for the most part, but that doesn't mean you need to look like you jumped off the cookie machine.

Have your own style and be confident about it. Notice I didn't say flamboyant. There's a difference.

Have some style and don't dress like a typical mathematician just to look like your environment, but know your limits. Remain professional with it.

The same is true for women. I would tell you not to dress too formal, too sexy, or too casual. I think women in this business should shoot for the middle ground and be fashionable, without going over the top.

What about a beard or mustache?

Well, women should have that waxed.

Men, I mean. (Almost unable to swallow her drink.)

(Hey, I need to have fun if I'm going to sit here for several hours, right?)

Men should do whatever makes them happy. But, I do think whatever it is should be neatly groomed.

In general, I say your overall appearance should be neatly groomed with clothes that are ironed, in good shape, and most of all, fit well.

So far, this all sounds great. It seems to be good advice for most people, not just loan officers.

I've always thought that loan officers have a tough job of, not just sales but, the technical side of sourcing the best financing and doing much of the detailed work most people wouldn't think they do. A professional loan officer could do well in any industry, I would think. So, what else do you want to teach loan officers?

Well, we've covered mindset and appearance. I'm also assuming that if loan officers need basic training, they've gotten it by now. Aside from the mechanics of being a loan officer, now I should probably cover getting business. After all, they will need to use their attitude and appearance when dealing with someone. Let's find that someone.

"If you want to cut the grass, there's only so much time you can spend trying to re-formulate the gas you put in the lawnmover. You can put bad gas in a mower and it will still run. Maybe not as smooth or as fast, but it will run. Mortgage education is the same way. You need to learn some fundamental basics and get straight talk from a mentor or teacher, but at some point you just need to get to cutting the grass. You learn the most pertinent lessons while you're actually doing the work.

Getting the Business
MARKETING

Okay, so I'm ready to move forward and I want business. Now what?

I know you want business. Lots of it.

The problem of marketing can be complex, so we need to break it down.

You need to develop clients. How to get them depends on you. You can rub elbows all over town, hand out cards to everyone you meet, pass out flyers or have them passed out, attend workshops and meetings, join a focus group, hire a marketing company, buy leads, and much more.

So which one do you think is the best to choose?

Well, you will want to do all of them at some point. I would normally say buy leads and tell everyone you meet what you do for a living. This hasn't changed much. Now, I would say enlist the help of an internet marketing partner, tell everyone you meet, and email or mail everyone you've ever met, telling them what you do. That way, you won't run into your Uncle Jerry in a few months, just after he did a loan with someone other than you.

That would be upsetting.

Well, it happens more than you might think. Loan officers are usually not the best at spreading the word about what they do to everyone they know, once getting into the mortgage business. You must cast a big net in a repeated and methodical way. Remember that this is a pipeline business. To build it takes time and it gets easier over time if you do it right. It's like an old manual water well pump. You must pump it for a long time for water to come out. Then, if you keep it going steadily, it's easy to keep it going. In the mortgage business, and in all other sales careers, all you really need to do is let people know what you do and that you care. Then, they will have the opportunity to ask you for help. If nobody knows what you do, nobody will ask for your help.

So what if I don't know an abundance of people?

Then it's time to start making friends and getting to know your market.

If you don't know your market, you should get to know it! Get out there, pass out cards and flyers, meet people, and go to functions. Nobody got anywhere waiting for the phone to ring. Well, maybe someone, but the odds are against it. Success doesn't usually happen unless you go out and grab it.

If you are new to the mortgage business, the aspect of the market you should concentrate on first depends on your skill set, sphere of influence, and where you have the best working knowledge. Your available target market consists of three basic types of prospects: first time homebuyers, refinance clients, and home equity, or debt consolidation, clients. Basically, you should look for people who are renting currently but don't want to, people who already own a house and want to pay less, and people who own a house and have gotten into trouble with debt. These different types of clients can be equally rewarding to help and present you with completely different motivations, concerns, and levels of homeowner experience. You wouldn't want to get into sharing some basic home maintenance tips with someone who has been in their home for ten years. Likewise, you wouldn't share a nightmare home maintenance tale with a new first-time homebuyer.

Your sphere of influence consists of: who you know and what kind of people you know.

Do you know doctors, young people, old people, car racing fans, or athletes? What people have you met through your previous jobs and personal relationships?

I've accumulated quite a large sphere of influence, but what if I didn't? What if I was a new loan officer, didn't know very many people, and didn't have a large sphere of influence?

You'd become a ghost writer.

(I said this playfully. As she folded her arms in front of her, I noticed a scowl coming.)

I'm just kidding. The one thing you need is an audience. So, if you don't have contacts, you need to buy them. You need either money or a database, and usually a little of both. The one section of the market I tend to recommend for new loan officers is first-time homebuyers.

If you don't know a lot of people and don't have a clearly defined sphere of influence then, perhaps, first time homebuyers would be a good target market. Think of this: neither of you know much about a home loan, you can relate to them, and they need guidance. I'd try to cultivate these type of contacts from renters rather than wooing realtors for referrals, which is a completely different ballgame. I don't know the name of the little man who teaches realtors to be mean and ugly to mortgage loan officers, but he's hard at work. Maybe it's in their training manual. I don't know what causes it, but I've never relied on realtors for business, which is unfortunate. I think we could make a great team if I could find some realtors with the right attitude.

To cultivate clients from renters you can sponsor a pool party at a local apartment complex, advertise a free weekly first-time homebuyer workshop, advertise with "why rent when you can buy," and do a side-by-side comparison of how equity grows versus throwing it away on rent. You can mingle at the local places where renters are likely to hang out and get involved in the community.

That way, you can become an expert at helping this group of people. Then, realtors will be looking to you for referrals. That's the way to get referrals from realtors. Give them business and, if they don't reciprocate, take it away from them and go to another one. Don't be at the mercy of a realtor for your business. They have too many loan officers hitting them up and they aren't likely to be loyal, unless you're giving them business consistently. However, there are exceptions to the rule. For instance, if you catch new realtors in school, you may develop a good alliance before they're misled by others, who have developed negative mortgage industry attitudes.

Okay, that's good. So, back to my big sphere of influence or past client database. How can I develop business from them?

That's the best client: a referral from another client. You can generate them from past clients or current ones. I recommend developing referrals from current clients, but any referral is a good lead. They almost never haggle about a deal if it's good and benefits them. Non-referrals haggle just because they've been told to. Referrals see you as the expert because you helped someone they know. So, you always need to nurture that and be careful not to take it for granted. Generate referrals before the loan closes with your clients. Always earn the right to ask for referrals and then ask for them before closing the sale.

How do you earn the right to ask for referrals?

By doing what you say you'll do. By being honest, even if you don't think they'll like what that may be. By working hard for your client, you earn the right to ask for future business from them and to ask them for referrals.

Okay, I understand. Please continue. How would I go about getting referral business from a client?

Up front, explain that you are going to ask for three referrals, after you prove yourself, because you want to spend more time on getting their loan closed and less time marketing.

Then, before the sale is done, just hand them a sheet of letterhead and say, "This is for those 3 referrals. I want you to know, I'll treat them with respect and will do my best to help them achieve their goals, just as I've done for you." Then, don't say a word. Remember, you earned it.

I love it! It's very bold but I can see how it would work. What about business cards?

Business cards are more than just your contact information. Most business cards look like all others and are boring. The ones that focus on benefits catch my attention. Instead of listing a few things you offer, try listing the benefits of what you offer. For instance, instead of saying you offer great rates, try saying you help people achieve their dreams of home ownership. Pass one out to everyone you meet. Remember, a conversation is better than, "Here is my business card if you ever need me." Try a more direct approach like, "Here's my business card, so how can I help make your life better today?" Also, don't hesitate to use brochures, one-sheets, or pamphlets to add to your print advertising. Keep them in your car for easy access. You never know when you'll get the urge to go prospecting.

I do think talking to someone before getting a business card would help me want to use that person. Just a business card is impersonal. Are there ways to get the same result without going out personally?

Sure. I remember, a few years ago I did a word-of-mouth campaign.

Here's how it works: get some college students passing out flyers and talking good about you, give them each a code so you know who referred who, and put a coupon on the flyers you give them with something like, "½ price origination fee… limited time offer."

Make it fun for the students and have pizza parties. Remember, you're the boss. Treat them well and have fun. They'll be enthusiastic about working with you and they'll learn that real business is conducted during fun. That's why you hear people say that a ton of business is conducted on the golf course. Real business happens with life, not outside it from a cold little cubicle in a dusty office building.

You can also reach many more people with a radio show. Arrange for a radio show spot or interview. There are hundreds of stations and shows in the market. You have to be doing something great, not just mediocre. Offer to talk straight about your industry, or service, and answer questions. With the expanded service of satellite radio, you have a limitless number of shows where you could be a guest speaker.

Okay, that's if I'm aggressive. What if I'm not? How about passive advertising, like newspaper and print ads?

Unfortunately, the less you're willing to work, the lower you should expect your results to be. Newspaper ads are not as effective as they used to be. However, if you make a big event out of your business endeavor, one which benefits society, send in a press release. You're likely to get a camera crew, or at least a columnist, to visit with you. They're always looking for a good story.

It sounds like I could really get the ball rolling with some interviews.

You're right. If you work hard, you can get good results. Most TV stations monitor radio station programming. Likewise, most radio stations monitor newspaper stories. Now, I know there are reciprocal relationships here so newspapers may monitor TV as well, but that's not my point.

One thing all of us need to do is to make our community a better place. For instance, organize a book donation party or drive to benefit schools and libraries in your area. You want to do things that are necessary, so call the school principals and libraries to find out what will make the most difference for them. Call your Mayor or Sheriff to get ideas for things you can do that help society in your area, and act on it. Send press releases to every newspaper, radio show, radio station, and TV station in your area. Newspapers and radio shows are always looking for content.

After you get the ball rolling with media, send notices to all the groups and businesses you can think of. Really make your event a big thing. Get people involved. Do it big while remembering to have fun.

When news media comes to you for an interview, you can state what kind of person you are. You can also relate your purpose to your business. You're a mortgage loan officer who just loves to help people.

Your purpose with the event is to help people. It's all about service to others. When you stop trying to sell a product or service and promote helping people, your sales come as a byproduct. The byproduct of your event becomes increased business for you and the feeling you get of accomplishment.

There's no shame in stating how you help people with their mortgage and how willing you are to help anyone listening or reading the article. Most everyone on this earth needs to work for a living. Promoting your business, while doing something charitable, is acceptable.

It sounds like you're leading up to something.

I am. Here's the point:

When you do good things, do them BIG. Then, promote them and get an interview with the news media. This gives you an opportunity to spread how good it feels to do something charitable, and beneficial, in the community. This is a feeling that prompts others to do the same. Other people will want to plan events that help the community when they see you having fun doing it, and becoming successful at the same time.

By shining brightly, you will attract others who will want to shine with you. Spreading how fun and rewarding it is to help others, can only perpetuate the efforts you began. You will do your part to better the community while increasing your client base at the same time. Your purpose should not be to gain personal gratitude or a pat on the back. You promote what you do as an act of good will so that others will want to do these kinds of things. It helps promote the spirit of charity. There's nothing wrong with that.

No, there's not. I think it's a great idea.

Do you have any others?

I have as many as you want. But, the ideas I want to teach are only the one's I've had success with and have seen others succeed with. I want to talk about just a few more in the book.

Fair enough. Tell me about them.

One is FSBO Marketing or For-Sale-By-Owner Marketing. In this campaign, you set appointments to speak with the sellers of for-sale-by-owner properties. When you meet with them, tell them your purpose is to help them sell their house faster by promoting it to your database, and on your website, free of charge.

Explain to them that you also help limit FSBO crimes by screening people before they view the house. If the children of a couple, whom they are showing the house to, are robbing the seller, while everyone is in a different part of the house, this is an example of a FSBO crime. Crimes that are much more violent can happen, and do happen, during the process of showing a house.

Think about it. The seller doesn't know the prospective buyers. They could be extremely bad people and nobody would know the difference. If you screen them and do a reverse lookup on their phone, you will have some indication about their honesty.

Tell the seller you want to pre-qualify everyone, no matter how messed up they think their credit is. By looking at everyone, you could help protect the seller and prevent them from wasting time.

You shouldn't show, or answer questions about, the house. You're there, at the request of the seller, to help screen and pre-qualify people. That's all.

There are many reasons to do this. Here are my notes on the benefits of FSBO marketing...

FSBO Multiple streams of business.

1. Provide financing for the person who buys the fsbo house.

2. Help those who didn't qualify by referring them to credit restoration.

3. Help seller with their new home loan.

4. Work with a realtor for the prequalified people who didn't get the fsbo home. This way you can give them referrals before asking for them in return.

Provide a yard sign and a few pre-qualification sheets to keep in the house. This will maximize your exposure.

There are tons of ideas about yard signs. I drew two for you in my notes…

JobsForLoanOfficers.com

WHY RENT WHEN YOU CAN BUY!

Get into this home
with little or no money down.

Joe Loanofficer
555-555-5555

Mortgage Company Name

Easy Prequalification

Honest Answers

CALL NOW FOR A
FREE LOAN CONSULTATION

Jill Loanofficer
777-777-7777

Next, I thought of a unique and inexpensive idea.

You can use another company's resources to promote what you do, and they'll like it.

It's called "Payroll marketing."

Employers are always looking for ways to provide more benefits and rewards to their employees, which helps morale and retention. Therefore, you'll help them do just that.

The way it works is that you will provide a specialized discount offer to employees of XYZ corp. inside their paycheck envelopes!

A small slip of bright yellow paper, in with employee paychecks, costs the employer nothing.

You provide however many slips the payroll department needs and they'll do the rest. The wording is up to you. You just want to make sure to follow compliance rules and regulations.

You also may need to meet with the business owner multiple times before they'll feel comfortable with you. It's well worth the time to get this idea working. You may pick companies of any size, but mid-size is best. Over 20 and less than 500 employees would be a good size company to start with.

I like that one! Very interesting. So they get their paycheck and see that you are offering to help them keep more of that paycheck by consolidating credit cards. Or, something like that?

Wow, you're catching on fast. How would you like to come work for me?

Not so fast... Although, I am intrigued by the intricacies of it, which I never thought about. I would have never known it was so involved.

It can be.

Let me tell you about my last topic on marketing for clients. If you remember I said that you must have either money or a database, or a little of both.

The way to really spend some money is to buy leads.

Who would you buy leads from? I mean, what's the best company?

You know, I really don't have a favorite, except maybe hot transfers. I dislike all of the rest for one reason or another. However, when I started out in the mortgage business, we had a computerized leads system.

It was a pool of interested people who were generated by telemarketers, television ads, or direct mail responses. We could see how old the lead was and call it.

If you call leads, as a loan officer, there are some things to keep in mind, which will help you make the best use of them.

Here's the list I've been making as we talked…

JobsForLoanOfficers.com

1. Call them promptly

2. GOAL = APPLICATION
Call 10 a day or take one app, then quit for the day.
Go home, etc.

3. Call from 5:30pm to 8:30pm if possible, and some Saturdays from 1pm to 4pm

4. Take breaks to play a game, have lunch, go shopping at the mall, etc. The key is to have FUN!

So, to wrap up this topic I'll just say that leads can be lucrative if you get good exclusive leads or hot transfers, follow my list of advice, and put everyone into a database for future use.

It sounds like it works, but only with a tremendous amount of effort.

Leads can be a tough way to go, unless you really spend a great deal of money for a quality leads system from a respectable company. It's definitely not my preferred way to generate business.

I can see that. So, let's say I do one or more of these plans and start getting business. Then what? About marketing, I mean.

That's a great question and one I was just starting to touch on.

After you get clients, it's important for you to know what else you can do to perpetuate your marketing efforts.

Sure, you treat the client right. But what else do you do?

Do you give the referring person a gift card with a thank-you note?

Do you call them in celebration of their closing or send them some cookies?

Do you take notes about your client's personal information such as spouse and child names, birthdays, graduations coming up, weddings, or other events for the purpose of recognizing them when one happens?

About purchase clients, do you send them a building-supply gift card, after closing, so they can get something nice for their new home?

What about Christmas cards, a birthday email, or a wishing-you-well note?

If you aren't doing things like this, you aren't "WOWING" your clients.

Or getting referrals I'd say.

Exactly! If you want referrals from your clients, you need to do more than make a good first impression. You need to stay in front of them all year long. Maybe you could give them useful information in a monthly newsletter or email. If you find that a client got a new job, call to congratulate them. You must develop quality relationships with your clients if you want to truly give unmatched service and be the one they turn to for mortgage help.

Like their family physician.

Yes, like the family doctor.

The best referrals are usually obtained during the sale process, not after. Think of this: people will like you best when you're solving their problems and working hard for them. Afterwards, you'll get a thanks and a pat on the back, but the sale is over and they're getting back to their daily routine. It's like a great book you read. While you're reading it, you're likely to tell your friends about it. A week after you finish the book, you're much less likely to tell anyone about it.

So, it's like you're old news for the most part?

Yes. Don't count on too many referrals after the sale is over. I like to explain to my clients that I mostly have a referral business that relies on my clients to provide my next client. This way I can spend more time on them and less time marketing. I tell them that I'm going to prove myself worthy and then I'm going to ask for a few referrals.

How do you prove yourself?

By telling them exactly what I'm going to do and then making good on that promise, and doing it. This is extremely important. Asking for referrals is a very personal thing for my clients. They guard their friends carefully, so you really need to gain their trust first. One thing I always do is explain things fully up front. I tell them what I'm going to do, then I do it, then I tell them what I did and ask for referrals before the sale is over.

It sounds simple.

Simple isn't always easy. You'd be surprised how hard some loan officers find this one thing is to implement. It requires confidence and courage to pull it off.

An easier, but less effective, referral technique is to tell the client, after the sale, that when they come across people who need help, to please call you directly and put you in touch with their friend or family member. Tell them not to simply give someone your number because it's likely they will never call. Have them actually call you and hand the phone to their referral.

If you can train your clients like that, you'll see some powerful things start to happen.

I read somewhere that the average business spends over six times more money to attract new customers than it does to keep old ones, which is unfortunate. Your past clients are a wealthy resource of potential leads and referral sources, but only if you maintain and manage your client database. Not having one, or not actively marketing to the one you have, means you could definitely be working smarter.

It seems like, with all of this to consider, I might get in my own way, and be indecisive. How would I overcome this?

Getting out of your own way can be hard, I admit.

To do it, you must focus on your primary task without thinking about it too much.

Your only goal is to help one person, with a mortgage loan, at a time. Once that one is set up and running, you can go get another one. Hopefully, you'll help a person who deserves it so you don't waste your time. Focus on one client, then another. So many times loan officers think they need 10 or 15 closings, for instance, so they don't do anything. The task seems too big.

So, I teach loan officers to focus on one at a time. Stop at nothing to get that one person. If people want to chat about things not pertaining to your goal, tell them that you'll have to get back to them later.

Move from place to place and person to person in search of one client to help.

Then another and another, but only one at a time until you reach your maximum client goal. Mine is twenty but yours can be whatever you want it to be.

This method should help you build business in a steady and predictable way.

You have to do to yourself what farmers do to their draft horses. Put blinders on so you don't get distracted from your goal of helping a client, a person.

I feel like I could go out and start helping people right now. You've given so many ways to do it. But, I find myself doubting that I could do it. Or, at least produce at any respectable level.

PUMP IT UP

It's interesting you say that. I was thinking about telling you about "pump it up."

Pump it up?

Yes, sales managers typically and routinely tell their people to "PUMP IT UP" at their meetings.

I've heard it many times over the years. But some salespeople silently say, "HOW?" and then end up unhappy with their careers because they couldn't answer that question or reach their potential.

I always say that it's simple but not easy. If that's the case, anyone can do it, it's just a matter of effort and direction. The direction part is important. Without it, you'd look like a balloon sputtering around the room after being blown up and let loose. This is the primary problem with "pump it up." No direction is given. They rely on sheer enthusiasm, which will burn out any sales force and require consistent hiring and firing.

Like running uphill against the wind.

More like running up a muddy hill in the rain, but I see you get the point.

Pumping it up the right way, with direction, is not rocket science. In martial arts, golf, and many other things in life, when you don't know what to do, the coach tells you to go back to the basics.

The trouble is that many loan officers were not properly taught the basics, so they were kind of "self taught." Teaching yourself is great, in some ways, and I don't want to change what they've learned during their struggles. It builds tough skin, character, and strength.

However, I do want to bring up some basics that have brought me, and my group, great success over the years.

10/20/10

Okay, so now this brings us to your notes on the basics. You have 10/20/10 written here. What does it mean?

It's my 10/20/10 approach. It's just another piece of the puzzle that relates to sales effort and prospecting. It can be modified for any particular goal, but 10/20/10 is simply this: do enough, per day, to have ten quality conversations about what you do, with someone new, five days per week.

Or, take one loan application, per day, five days a week. Now, this means a real deal, not a mind deal. A mind deal is one that you put together which has very little chance of closing, with a borrower who really isn't committed to doing business with you.

When I was a new loan officer, I forced myself to have ten new conversations, about a loan, with someone new, every workday, or I took one application. It was either/ or. If I had two conversations and my third produced an application, I took the rest of the day off. Usually, I went home because I called out from 5:30PM to 8:30PM. If I got my application at 6:00PM, I went home early. Then, the first part of the next day was dedicated to organization and task planning. I called my mornings a quiet time. It was the perfect time to contemplate, plan, prioritize, and pray. The middle of the day I reserved for raw work on the deals I had in process, starting with any new application I received the night before. So, after about 10:30AM I would process my files.

What if I work hard, have ten conversations a day, and don't get any applications?

No sweat. The numbers will take care of themselves. It's impossible for you to stick with this plan for two weeks and not get any applications.

Impossible?

Impossible. Think about it. Do you really think you can speak to 100 qualified leads and not get a sale? That's why I say it's impossible. Maybe it would be better to say "extremely unlikely."

You've got a point. Okay, so that looks like the 10 part of the 10/20/10. What's the next part?

OK, the second part of 10/20/10 is this: twenty loans in your pipeline at all times. I know it sounds like a bunch, but remember your goal is success not mediocrity. Work up to 20 and then maintain it. Utilize a good processor and do it. If you're going over your goal of twenty working loans, and feel overwhelmed, stop and only do the ten conversations a few times per week, or even once a week. I got to where I did it once a month after my fourth month on this plan. If I can do it, anyone can. I hate cold calling. But, remember you're only getting the word out about what you do and who you are. Your goal is not to sell in the broad use of the word. If you offer something good and it helps people, it sells itself. You're just the messenger to show people why it's good and how it helps. People can make up their own minds to buy or not to buy. That's sales. Most people think of sales as the crafty hard-core salesperson using scare tactics and other methods of persuasion to get clients to buy. Sales only needs to be crafted and scripted if you're selling something people don't need. Providing a good solution, to a real need, sells itself and only needs to be promoted.

So, are you saying that anyone can sell if they're representing a thing that benefits people or solves a real problem?

Exactly!

So, moving along, if you do this as you should, making enough calls to have ten conversations or one loan application per day five days per week, a surprising thing happens. After just one week, either you'll have talked to fifty brand new people, who need your services or know others who do, took five loan applications, or somewhere in between. You'd be well on your way to the goal of twenty loans in your pipeline.

Doing this will spread your word to about three hundred people per month, over three thousand per year.

Do three thousand people know what you do for a living?

I don't know. Probably not.

Also, this is just for a consistent effort over a one year period.

Most loan officers couldn't say three thousand people know about them over their entire careers!

Can you imagine the snowball effect of referral business coming in from an extra three thousand people per year, who know what you do, and know how to get in touch with you?

It sounds amazing. Almost too good to be true.

It's not. It's simple and it works. Most people in sales do such a poor job promoting themselves that they can't get to this level even in five years. How's that for a reality check?

This brings us to the last part of this 10/20/10 method, which is the end goal. If you'll notice each of these numbers is a goal. The first is ten conversations; the next is twenty loans in your pipeline. Now this last piece is the real goal and one you can take to the bank.

You will be able to count on ten closed loans per month, minimum!

Standard gross earnings on a $150,000 loan are about $3000. But, whatever the actual numbers are, for any particular loan officer, simply multiply by ten. That's what you would be able to count on month in and month out, if you follow this plan.

The best part about it is that it doesn't take any special talent to be successful using this. You just do it and the numbers work themselves out in your favor. The main objective is just to do it.

JobsForLoanOfficers.com

"The KEY is to stay consistent"

"Structure your day and
enjoy your life.
The two go hand in hand."

10/20/10 RECAP

1. 10 conversations or 1 app
per day, 5 days per week.

2. Go through every file every
day, and do everything possible
on it.

3. DON'T SELL

EDUCATE and offer to HELP

It sounds like it would be simple to follow your plan.

It's simple, but not easy. It requires dedication and work.

So, how would I keep up with all of the people I talked to every day? I would want to recycle them somehow to make the most of my conversations, wouldn't I?

I think you're catching on.

I used an excel spreadsheet that I created with the prospect's contact information, the type of financing they wanted, and the outcome of the call. Then I used my calendar to schedule callbacks or follow-ups.

That way, my calling was done when the sheet was full each day. These days, you can use a contact management program. But, the old way works well and requires no updates, or computers, once the sheet is printed out.

This should help you immediately and for the rest of your career.

EFFORT LEVEL

My career?

I can see you getting excited about it. You're thinking about working with me, aren't you?

Who wouldn't? The way you explain it, it seems so easy and lucrative.

Ah, but remember I said it was simple... not easy.

I remember, I think you keep saying it.

I say it often because loan officers tend to get so excited about things that they forget the work part.

I'm not trying to boast here, but to state the facts, and illustrate a point, I'll tell you something. I was successful when par rates were at nine percent and we charged five discount points on every loan, for good or bad credit borrowers, and I wasn't over charging. It was simply the market rates at the time, and the program my company was offering.

I did it month after month and even won awards for the top sales production in a company with thousands of salespeople nationwide.

I was sent on trips with the red carpet rolled out everywhere I went. There weren't very many of us and we were treated like royalty.

I've often wondered why we were honored like that, and why there were so few of us. I think it was because it really required consistently hard effort to stay on track, and that achieving the numbers we did was far above average.

Soon after all of that, I was promoted to AVP and I trained loan officers how to do what I had done. I attribute it to a very good mentor, this 10/20/10 concept, and my PDF; my persistence, determination, and faith.

Also, I was thinking with so many things to consider, in addition to focusing, I would need to have a real motivation. Something that made me want to sincerely wake up in the morning and talk to people.

If you want the motivation to get up, get a really loud alarm clock.

Okay you don't need to be rude.

(I could see a little smile from Amelia and that she realized it was the truth.)

No, really. I've given you tons of motivation here. You must ultimately find your own underlying reasons for what you do. Getting up in the morning is between you and your maker. But, if you're going to endeavor to do this you must do it with purpose.

I always say if you're going to go to the party...SHOW UP!

What does that mean?

It means that if you're going to do something, do it in a big way. Do things in a way that gets attention and a way that makes a difference. If you don't intend to be a serious player in the game, you might as well stay home.

It sounds a bit harsh.

Hey, sometimes the truth hurts. It would do you absolutely no good for me to sugarcoat or hide the truth. But, I say it with a smile don't I?

It doesn't make it any easier to hear.

I know, but I don't have the luxury of being hurtfully polite, leading you into unknown territory without some hard advice. Mediocrity breeds all kinds of self-built hurdles, things you could avoid by just giving it all you have. When it's time to work, work; when it's time to play, play hard.

Do life with passion.

Why are you so passionate, well, about being passionate?

I think, early on, I heard that anything worth doing is worth doing well. I decided to adopt that philosophy but it took a while. A bunch of little things happened in my life that taught me lessons. Most of them centered around the efficiency of effort. Getting the most from the least amount of time investment requires hard work in intervals.

A member of my team once told me about an experience he had in high school football, and how it helped him in sales.

One of his coaches told him, "If you come off the field and have even one ounce of energy left, you didn't give it 100%." It's one of those quotes that will stick in your head as if it was yesterday.

That one sentence really changed his attitude towards his effort level. You can relate that quote to anything in life, not just football. It does, however, make you realize that you can't look at what you've done and say you gave it your all when you could have probably given it more. Coaches have a way of cutting to the heart of things.

So do you.

I'm sorry, but I have more on the subject of effort level, and how it relates to success. You can chastise me later.

If sitting around waiting for your phone to ring is considered a 1 on the effort level scale between 1 and 10, you can expect to be a loan officer at 1 on a success scale of 1 to 10 at that effort level.

"When you've gone so far that you can't manage one more step, then you've gone just half the distance you're capable of."

Greenland Proverb

What this quote means to me is simple.

When you think you've exhausted all efforts in marketing your mortgage business, think again.

If you really look at what you've done and chart the effort, and progress, you've made, you'll most likely find you haven't done everything you convinced yourself you did. Or, maybe you didn't do it as well or as consistently as you think you did.

Also, on the flipside, you will probably see a chartable progress you didn't notice before.

For instance, when you think you haven't had any success but you've been working 12 hours a day. Then, when you really think about it you realize, for example, you made several industry contacts, pre-qualified five people in the past week who are looking for houses, and you wrote an article for the local paper. Also, when you think about the 12-hour days, you realize that a good chunk of it was spent doing other personal things like surfing the web or looking at online auctions.

Time wasters will convince you that you spent that time working. That's why I try to limit my personal use of the computer to after hours. Otherwise, I'll be there for a few hours during the day and my memory will tell me it was work time when I can see clearly it was not.

I think 12-hour days would burn me out. Is it really necessary to work that hard?

I'm glad you caught that. No, it's not; not all the time, but sometimes it can be necessary.

It is better to work hard, with a passion, and take a distinct break, than to work moderately hard and take no breaks. Your actual productive time is pretty sparse when you drag out your tasks.

You need to work hard with a drive and purpose, then go somewhere and become a vegetable. Or, just remove yourself from all concerns or plans and have quality time with your family.

I spoke to a friend the other day, who felt like he was so tired that he needed a vacation. I asked what his days were like and if he ever took time for himself.

He said he woke up in the morning, had some coffee and read the newspaper. He said that was his time. He was wrong. That was not his time. That was time to flood his brain with all the crud going on in the world. That was time to crowd his task list with thoughts about what the stock market was doing, the latest advertisement for a new SUV, and governmental controversies. That was not a break.

A better break would have been to have a V-8, turn on some good music and write his thoughts in a journal. Getting your thoughts and cares out of your head is essential.

Just as planning your day, before you actually take any calls, is essential.

In America, we're so conditioned to melt everything together, that we forget how rich things are when we leave them apart. This is as true in planning your day as it is for leaving a culture alone, preserving its tradition and colorful heritage. A Chinese parade would look pretty funny with bagpipers in it, for example. Keep things separate and meaningful.

So, to sum it up?

To sum it up, work hard and then unplug your brain during your breaks. You'll be much more successful.

That's good advice I need to take. You know, as I'm sitting here, I think it sounds so simple, but as I learn more I realize it's complicated at the same time. It's a very strange paradox. As you said, it's simple but not easy.

Don't underestimate your potential success. Just jump in with both feet and do it!

Here's another quote for you. My friends call them "Billisms."

Billisms?

Yes, I don't know whether to be proud or embarrassed. I come up with advice to myself, which comes out like quotes. Then I share them with my friends. I guess

I'm happy they value what I say. Anyway, here's one I wrote down for you…

JobsForLoanOfficers.com

"Remember when we were young and were told to color inside the lines?

You're all grown up now, it's your world. Live in it.

SCRIBBLE ALL OVER THE PLACE!"

Getting outside the box can be tough. Why do you think it's so hard for people to do that?

I have an opinion about why I think it happens. Many times, in our lives, we sell ourselves short. This is for a variety of reasons but most likely because of our upbringing and schooling. We were taught how to do things the way they've always been done and to stay within preset boundaries. This is great as background knowledge to use as a springboard to new ideas, but not as a place to stop. More progressive teaching is what you would expect if you were a Rockefeller child, or a Forbes, Hilton, Gates, Trump, or from any progressive, philanthropic, family. My parents taught me to think big and that I could achieve anything. These basic ideas stuck with me even through the toughest times. These ideas, along with love and encouragement, gave me an advantage many people don't get. I expanded on these ideas to create and mold who I have become. Struggling and never giving up went a long way in teaching me the lessons to do just that. There's something special about what you learn from extremely hard effort over a prolonged period of time. As many older people have told me my whole life, hard work really does build character.

It seems like you initiated a paradigm shift in yourself.

Well, I don't know if I initiated it or if it was just necessary and happened, but I did have to make a conscious decision as to which road I was going to choose. You could say that I decided to go on a never-ending quest of personal growth, even though it seems to be the harder choice.

You have to break the traditional mold and realize that great people achieve greatness by inventing their own business models, and plans of action, or emulating and expanding on those of another successful person. A good college education should equip you for a corporate job or profession. It can also give you wonderful background knowledge to use as that springboard I was talking about. However, the college-taught ways of doing things don't usually promote entrepreneurship or innovation to principle. Now apply that kind of entrepreneurial spirit to our industry. Instead of placing some ads in the newspaper, bribing a few realtors with boxes of cookies, or passing out cards and flyers, think outside the box. Think of an angle nobody else is gutsy enough or creative enough to invent. Dare to be an innovator. Do what most people won't do, to have what most people don't have.

When I was a new loan officer, after I learned the basic standard way of marketing and doing loans, I started thinking that there simply must be a better way to do it. I started writing down truths. Such as, "going after a lead source will reap much more business than going after the end consumer," or "Most realtors are fickle and will throw you away for the next loan officer bringing a better brand of doughnuts." Things like that.

I weighed the odds of each decision and each lead source. I had decided that advertising to, or going after, lead sources, was the key. I don't remember exactly how I went about that, but I made a ton of calls for information. I soaked up everything I learned or heard and then looked for the thread of truth or the trend to what I was hearing. Then I could forecast what was going to happen or what I would most likely find in the process.

Where you would most find success.

Right.

Well, I started calling these companies that buy houses. I called the ugly house buyer people and picked a few brains. The selling point being, that instead of them carrying all of their notes and selling them for a percentage of their money, I wanted to try to get them all of their money. They liked my drive and persistence but their business model mandated a quick deal. Or, maybe they were just impatient. I did a few purchase loans for their buyers and they ended up being extremely hard to please. They wanted instant gratification and didn't appreciate me lecturing them on patience in exchange for more revenue.

Then, one day, I called a smaller operation buying about ten houses per month. Through multiple meetings, and creatively planning for them to yield more money, I was able to get them on board. I ended up being in their offices, much of the time, training all of their people on how to send me better deals, the best pre-qualifying questions to ask, and such. My manager wondered where I was all day and I had to really answer for myself on it. But, I cultivated that one company, increasing their revenue, and ended up receiving as many as six applications a day from them. I closed over thirteen loans per month from that one relationship. That's what made me one of the top loan officers in my company and helped me move up the ladder very quickly.

My point is this. I found the angle that was a win-win situation for everyone involved. The borrower got a better deal, the investor got all of their money, and I got plenty of business. Now this specific example would have to be modified for today's market, since title vesting is harder and the market is changing. But, it can still be done. They can turn their money over and buy more houses, which, in turn, will generate more business for you.

It certainly sounds like you thought outside the box. How did your employer feel about this unconventional way of attracting business?

They weren't very understanding at first. It wasn't a traditional way of doing things and I had to go to the top in my company for the approval to work these deals the way I wanted. The point is that I ended up breaking the mold. We all need to think outside the traditional lines and be smart, creative, and motivated to find a way to achieve what we want. Don't just do things you've been taught. Be persistent. Be hard-core. Be bold.

Bold. Hard-Core?

Bold as in, opening your mouth when you'd really rather keep quiet.

Not long ago, I met a man at the sporting goods store and decided to open my mouth. I asked what he did for a living. Then I told him what I did. As it turned out, he was having a house built and it was almost finished. The total cost was $950,000 and he was giving five percent down. He told me about the deal he was quoted and I thought it was a little too expensive. He was having to pay two discount points and he still had a high rate. I told him my thoughts, gave him a business card, and asked for his. Then, I told him to let me see if I could save him some money and that I would call him in the morning with a few ideas about what I found out. He gave me the information I needed and I wrote it on a napkin.

I just looked at standard programs for him that night. As it turned out, with the deal he was offered, I would have made four percent commission on that loan. That's a whopping $38,000 in revenue.

I found a good program, lowered my revenue a little and saved him over $400 per month, compared to the deal he was getting with the other broker. Also, with my equity acceleration program, he would save over $700,000 in mortgage interest. Plus, he got to shake my hand and look me in the eye. That goes a long way with people like him. I have no doubt why I got that deal.

Why?

Because I opened my mouth.

In other words, go outside your comfort zone.

Not just that. It's more. It's not enough to just open your mouth as much as possible. You also have to show you care and be prompt. Doing this will cause success to happen, the way it did for me, more than you realize.

It's also a lesson in the benefits of targeting Jumbo business. I'm really not jumping off the point but this reminds me of something you probably already know.

When I was in High School, the prettiest girls didn't always have things to do on the weekend. I found out that some of the prettiest girls in my school almost didn't get asked to the prom! Why?

Because every guy was too intimidated by our beauty to ask us out?

You joke, but you know it's true.

I found out in college, when I actually talked to a few girls about this in my study group. It just came up one day when I said they must have been hounded by guys in high school. A few of them told me that it was really upsetting and that they just went places with their parents, on the weekend, or stayed home. They weren't being asked out! That was a handy piece of information, after the fact, I wished I had known.

Okay, I know you're going to tell me, so how does that relate to mortgages?

It's the same with Jumbo and multi-million dollar loans. Many of these people get bad deals because there's not as much competition in that market. Big loan clients intimidate loan officers.

This man in my illustration was going to pay much more than necessary because someone had the guts to go after that kind of business.

I took it away by having the confidence to challenge the other lender, giving the man a fair deal, and saving him money. You can do fewer loans, spend more time with your clients, and make the same amount of money. Don't be afraid to rub elbows with wealthy people. In fact, some will become good friends. Also, wealthy people tend to have wealthy friends.

Now that's a circle I'd like to be a part of.

You could already be a part of it and don't even know. There's a saying, in these circles, that money doesn't talk about money. So you'll never know. I just treat everyone the same while I'm looking for larger loan amounts.

5 Cs of mortgage

1. Cash -- How much savings and income

2. Credit -- Do they have the credit strength to qualify?

3. Collateral -- Is the property something you would lend on, if you used your own money?

4. Capacity, -- Can they afford what you're doing for them!

5. Character -- Have they paid debts well in the past?

Look at the difference in pay history of house, car, and credit cards.

Now that you have a client... WHAT NEXT?

Okay, I don't mean to change the subject, but your notes pretty much run out here and move to loan origination.

You're right. I've talked long enough about marketing.

Now that you have a client, it's important to get good information from them.

Information is the key to successfully originating a loan. You need to know who, what, where, when, why, and how. This means: who are the borrowers, what kind of deal is it, where is it, when does it need to be completed, and why does the borrower want to do this kind of loan? I made some notes to illustrate some of the keys to evaluating a client. It's the "5 Cs" of mortgage.

Today's market is injured because more loan officers didn't ask these types of questions.

So you act like a bank underwriter?

I act as a pre-underwriter to at least try to make sure the deal is clean. You don't want to be a part of a fraudulent loan, so you simply ask questions up front. Plus, you can usually tell if someone will be approved or not, just by your conversation. You can only do this if you've had a thorough conversation.

Where do you have that conversation?

In person or over the telephone?

Either one.

DEVELOPING RAPPORT

I'd like to say some things about meeting a client in person.

First of all, you want to be on time, or a few minutes early. You should be calm and confident. If you're not calm, or confident, there are tools you can use to help get you in that state of mind. I know it sounds quirky, but I like some of the positive thinking and personal magnetism audio programs. They help me scrub the negative thoughts out of my mind and replace them with good thoughts.

If you do this all the time, it gets easier. There are times when I only need to close my eyes and focus on a few phrases to achieve a fresh state of mind. It's much easier to handle clients in a calm and confident way. They react better.

Phrases like what?

Things like: focus on their benefit, I'm only here to educate and help, and I'm the best at what I do. Things like that.

Okay, but how do I handle a client who is really tough to talk to, like a CEO type?

That's no problem, at least not when you realize they put their pants on the same way everyone else does. Don't place so much importance on how they act. You're there to give a good service to them. Just focus on that. You can't control what they do.

Okay, that's the general answer. Can you go into more detail?

Of course!

First, when trying to get your point across, you want to give it from within yourself, without all the clutter of your mind messing it up. Most of the time, the point you're trying to make is clouded by your fears about talking with someone or addressing someone in a position of power; someone you may be intimidated by. I like to use a concept I call the Break-Build Concept. I use it not only in my business but also in my personal life. It's particularly effective when introducing yourself, or pitching an idea, for the first time.

So you use sales methods in everyday personal life?

Sales is for life, not just for business. Any time you present yourself or an idea to someone, you're selling. You know how important initial impressions are. This is an opportunity for you to introduce yourself, become unforgettable, make your point, and earn the respect of the people you're addressing.

The CEO type of person I call a *type-A* person. *Type-A* is a behavior pattern. It's a set of characteristics such as being aggressive, competitive, impatient, excessively time-conscious, insecure, overbearing, highly driven, and sometimes hostile. These people are stressed-out most of the time and they feel the need to control everything. I think I see this type of person more than I'd like to, in the mirror.

I knew it! I was going to ask if you are this type of person, but I didn't want to offend you. Although, I think you're much more complex than that.

I believe I am. Since I try to never be put into a box or confined to a set of characteristics.

Okay, I'm sorry. Please continue about meeting these types of people.

Well, as soon as you enter the room of your meeting, make a quick assessment as to who the decision maker is, and likely the controlling *type-A* personality. If you're only meeting with one person, try to determine if they have a *type-A* personality. It's important for you to always evaluate your audience so you can better get your point across. You can do this by asking a few open-ended questions and then just listening to the client talk.

God gave us one mouth and two ears because He meant for us to listen twice as much as we talk.

Another Billism?

Nope. This is a "Texasism." I've heard it several times but only from native Texans. So, maybe it came from here. Even if it didn't, I like it.

I like it too. So, what are the details of the client meeting?

The basic procedure for a meeting starts with being cordial. Then, meet and introduce yourself to everyone involved, paying attention to introduce yourself to the *type-A* person first. This will likely be the one introducing you, unless it's a subordinate introducing you to the business owner, or person in charge. I told you this can be tricky.

I can see that. It's quite intriguing.

Always thank them for their time and move to begin the meeting, unless they have upfront questions for you.

After that, begin by telling them about yourself, and the company you represent. Be brief about yourself and always speak from your heart, especially now. This will let them know your level of passion for what you do, and it gives them a window into your character.

If you have experience, tell them about it. If you don't, then focus on what's really important. What's important is that you're there to help them and intend to focus fully on doing just that. A few credibility lines about your company help, but remember what your goal is; to help them, so move quickly to that.

You don't have to talk about yourself much. After you give them a few short facts about you, and the company, then the logical progression would be to introduce the ways you can help them. I like to do this by first educating them about some of the false information they may have been given, or may be given in the future. I make it clear to my clients that, even if they don't use me, I want them to have good information.

THE BREAK – BUILD CONCEPT

So, after you evaluate the room and handle introductions, what is the "break- build" concept you mentioned and that I see in your outline?

The Break-Build Concept is a method of giving and taking away control, in order to better teach, while taking charge of the meeting.

Recently, I consulted with an instructor of a combat martial arts system about how to present his training to the government. During our meeting, I talked about the natural progression of presenting his training in a way that they could understand it. His training was unlike any I had ever seen, so it was easy for him to point out less useful and less effective training methods, normally taught by other instructors. I decided to illustrate my point to him using the concept of shoving an attacker's nose into his brain with the palm of the hand, which is, unfortunately, a widely taught method for women to use in confrontation with an attacker. However, it's pretty much ineffective since the precision of targeting, and the force of impact, is directly related to the success or failure of this technique. It's unlikely someone inexperienced could use it well. So, I told him to use that as one of the illustrations of what is ineffective.

That doesn't work? I just learned it a few months ago in a self-defense class.

I wouldn't rely on it. Just use your palms, instead of fists, with fingers up. Hit with your palms, driving forward, and use your fingernails for eye attacks. If the attacker can't see you, he's less likely to continue his attack. Plus, I can imagine it would hurt quite a bit.

Okay. Wow. Thank you.

No problem. But, back to my meeting.

While showing my friend how to present his art, I had a revelation of sorts and realized that my instruction to him was the same as the art of the sale itself. I told him to present his ideas from his heart, without his brain clouding the whole thing.

While I did this, I calmly approached him, getting very close with my tone getting a bit louder, making my point, and then calmly backing off and making my concluding point or question much softer, to let the main point soak in. It was like squeezing a sponge so that more water could be soaked up.

He said it made him feel my excitement and it made him just a little uncomfortable, at first. Then, as I backed off and the point soaked in, as I intended, he felt good about it.

Now that I've opened your mind to this, you'll notice, more easily, when someone does it. Most of the time, it's by design.

I realized, while teaching this to him, that it wasn't the first time I had used this technique. It occurred to me that I use this method very often with people.

It was extremely effective breaking him down a little, by making him slightly uncomfortable, and then, when the idea was complete, backing off to let him own it. Thus, building him back up again.

It sounds like a powerful tool to have.

This is so powerful that, when you master it, people will sometimes think your point was their idea. This concept is widely used by people who may not even know they're using it. I decided to adopt it as part of my instruction here because it's one of those things nobody ever offers to teach. It's unlikely many even really understand it.

This concept is for meeting with one, two, or a group of people. But, there are other things to consider if you're in a group.

Very interesting. I saw you use it, while talking about it, sitting in a chair. From your explanation, I didn't think it would work sitting down.

It's not supposed to. But, thank you. It's something I hadn't thought about.

So tell me about how you use it in a group.

When you start your presentation in front of multiple people, you must address the *Type-A* person first. Pay particular attention to look them straight in the eyes when doing this, as in the introduction phase.

Then, take your attention away from *Type-A,* and focus for a minute on each person in the room, if possible.

I never thought about that. I thought I was just supposed to focus on the decision maker.

This is very important!

Never leave out the "mouse in the corner." Always address them with just as much respect as the *Type-A* person, but with one difference. Never use the Break-Build technique with anyone who is not a strong personality type. You only want to build them up.

Mouse in the corner?

The "mouse in the corner" is, for instance, a quiet spouse not wanting to get involved or steal the spotlight from the *Type-A* spouse.

Why would you focus on someone who doesn't want any attention?

That's a wonderful question.

If you thought you were supposed to give all of the attention to the decision maker, you're dead wrong.

What happens when you take your gaze from *Type-A*, and focus on others, is very complicated and lengthy in its entirety, but I'll try to explain in simple terms.

When you focus on the softer personalities in the room, you give them something. Do you know what it is?

Respect?

Yes. Something they probably don't get often. It's the "mousey" person who usually just sits quietly in the corner and listens, never having a say and never getting attention. Sometimes they do it out of fear and lack of self-respect. You will change that, even if it's in a small way. This is empowering to others and it's something you should do in every area of your life.

Always try to build people instead of letting them continue to be left out of the decision making process.

I'll bet it also stirs up the decision maker.

Absolutely. Something else happens with *Type-A* and it's important that it happen. It, once again, is the manifestation of the Break-Build Concept. You purposely take the limelight away from *Type-A*, and give attention to the weaker person in the room. This, like getting close to *Type-A*, makes them feel uncomfortable.

But, you don't want to make a potential client angry, do you?

This isn't bad…it's good!

You don't let them feel uncomfortable too long, otherwise they would get angry. You should focus on *Type-A* again with the same passion and respect you had when you started.

So, give and take respect, and attention, away from the Type-A person twice?

Exactly!

Well, not just twice, but as many times as it takes. Guess what? Congratulations, you just took control of the meeting.

This let's *Type-A* know that you're in charge of the conversation but have the respect and class to involve everyone in the room, not just them in particular.

Most salespeople will continue to focus on the *Type-A* person out of fear and because it's easier to do. They don't want to "break the rice paper." I sometimes refer to this as "walking on eggshells," as you have probably heard before.

If that's what you've been told to do, throw away that advice. Don't do it. You will be run over by these people if you don't take control of the situation and let them know you're not only intelligent, respectful and cordial, but also strong and confident.

Once you've gained control over the situation, you continue to Break-Build with *Type-A,* and continue to show you care about the others involved, getting their opinions and views on things, as well.

Then, always go back and focus on *Type-A* to remedy the breaking you did, no matter how small. Never leave anyone feeling defeated.

What if the decision maker has misconceptions about something, like a rate or program they think they can get, and you know them to be wrong?

Never challenge *Type-A* in front of others. You can do this, if needed, in private. But, never, under any circumstances, engage *Type-A* in a power match in front of people. You'll belittle them and lose your relationship.

For instance, what if *Type-A* is being doubtful about what you're presenting, bringing up a misconception you mentioned, trying to engage you or stump you?

If this happens, you should take back control by not losing your cool, instead of throwing it in their face. Always keep calm. It exudes confidence and continues to impress people with your professionalism and strength.

Acknowledge their concerns and find out where they learned that piece of information. Be as pleasant as possible when you give accurate information or handle the objection, but in no way allow them to continue thinking something that is untrue. It's a much more professional way to handle an objection than hitting them in the nose with it in front of their spouse or employees. Instead of getting defensive, get caring and creative. If you truly care about your client, you will use your passion for helping them as a means to consult with them, rather than just trying to make a sale.

They learn something that way also, I would think.

Yes, and if you educate them in the process, it's even better.

My best clients go away from our very first meeting knowing much more about what I'm offering than anyone ever dared to teach them. I look at a sale in this way: if I use old school, "used car," tactics to land the sale, they may indeed buy from me. But, I doubt if they will respect me, or anyone in my industry, afterwards. They will certainly not refer people to, or tell their friends and family about, me; not in a positive way. On the contrary, they'll most likely tell their friends and family about it in such a way that I'll never get business from them, or anyone they know.

If you go into it caring about them with your purpose being to educate and help them, it's likely they'll buy from you, thank you, and tell others.

Now that you've made your introductions and created a favorable rapport, now what do you do?

After you've explained who you are, who your company is, what you have to offer, and why it's good for them, it's time to ask for the sale. Something like, "Okay, now I believe I've adequately explained who I am, who I represent, and that my service is clearly superior to most out there, I see no reason why we shouldn't get started doing business together." Then shut up.

Say nothing?

Literally, say nothing. Do not say a word after you've made a bold statement like that. Just smile a little and look at each party in the room. Sitting at the table with my client, I'll make a statement like that with the application in front of them and holding out a pen for them to take and sign the paperwork. I say nothing until they break the silence. Usually they sign if the deal makes sense and is good for them.

How long have you had to stay silent, in the past?

A very uncomfortable two minutes, or so. My client looked at his wife, looked through the disclosures a few times, looked at my face and even looked at his watch. It was funny too because I could almost hear the music from an old western that plays at the beginning of a duel.

It sounds like you could sell them just about anything like that.

You could. But, let me tell you, if you're selling something that's not good for your client, or you intend to take advantage of them in any way, quit and find a different job.

There's absolutely no reason to use scare tactics, and tired old cheesy methods, to close a sale and charge a big fee. It's unethical and against our duty to God and society. Only sell a product or service you can be proud of, and have a passion for selling. Anything else will put you into an uncomfortable situation and tempt you to compromise your values for money. Never lower yourself to hurt someone, no matter how minor you think it is, for money. It's just not worth it.

You sound pretty passionate about that. Why?

I am dearly passionate about this for many reasons, but I'll give you one. I got out of the car business, the used car business in particular, because I saw way too much dishonesty and greed. I got into the mortgage business so I could help people get into a home of their own, and get their kids out of the apartment scene. What I found was worthwhile and made me feel good at the end of the day. We help people better afford their home, pay off revolving debt, and get that land they want to build their dream home on. We help the business owner expand and real estate investors obtain homes, duplexes, and apartment buildings. Notice, in everything we do…we help. Helping people is the single most rewarding thing you will ever do, while living your short time here on Earth.

That's touching. Do many salespeople feel the way you do?

I think many do. I hope many do.

I hope so too.

I'm sorry to skip around here but back to rapport building. Can you do it if you aren't there in person?

You can and I do. You have to find common ground and listen more than you speak. Ask the client open-ended questions and really listen to the answers.

That's really it. Just be concerned about what their needs are and ask lot's of probing questions. Let them know you want to give them an educated response based on real facts, not empty promises. Tell them what you're going to do, do it, and then remind them what you did, just like we discussed earlier.

JobsForLoanOfficers.com

Beleviee me wehn I say taht
plpoee dnot crae waht oredr
you use, nor do tehy uesdnatnrd
eunogh to crae. Tehy jsut wnat
you to hlep tehm.

THE INITIAL INTERVIEW

This is really very interesting. But, I still don't feel like I know enough. What's the most important thing that I would need to know before getting started as a loan officer?

First of all, you will never know everything about anything. If you wait until you know everything, you'll starve. The most important thing you need to know is how much you want to help people. You can ask yourself that question.

Next to that, a good thorough interview, and conversation, is necessary. You can take the loan application from your notes or while you're talking to your clients. But, you don't want taking the loan application to be more important to you than the conversation and interview. You should be able to take a good application during your conversation. Most of the time, I take notes while I'm talking to a client, and then create the application from my notes. That way, I'm more focused on them than the application form.

If you don't use the application form, how do you know what to ask?

Experience teaches you that. You can start by looking at all the items on a loan application.

Keep these things in mind:

What do they want to achieve with this financing?

Where do they live?

Where do they work?

What do they make?

How much money do they have saved up?

Then just expand on each of those. Find out what's important to them and what their objectives are. Learn as much as you can about them and their goals, then you'll know what to ask.

If you care about them, you'll ask the right questions. It doesn't matter what order you go in, just make sure you get all of the important information.

If I'm a new loan officer, what if I don't know the answers to a client's questions?

First, don't be nervous. Just smile and tell them you don't know but you'll find out. Then write a note to yourself about it. If it's a deal killer, excuse yourself from the conversation and call someone right then. Having a mentor can be extremely beneficial.

But, I wouldn't want to come across as being stupid.

They won't think you're stupid. Remember, I said you'll never know everything.

Just be sincere and let them know you will find out. Someone once told me that people generally don't care how much you know, they just want to know how much you care. It's true.

There seems to be a tremendous amount of information to know to be good at this.

If you don't know if you could ever be good at this, you're normal. But, I know that you will!

Certainly, you will. Just care enough about your client to educate them about what to watch out for, what the real process is, and what you're willing to do for them.

Then, let them know that, whether they use your services or not, they must have the truth about how things are done. Most of the time, they'll respect the honesty and confidence it took to have that conversation with them, and they'll use you.

It's true, I don't see too many really honest salespeople these days. But, I've noticed a few different types. I wouldn't want to be the type who would say or do anything just to get a sale. So, how do you sell with honesty?

You never need to compromise yourself to get a sale. If the program solves a problem or helps people achieve their objectives, just propose it to them. If they like it, great, if not, move on.

How do you handle objections such as people saying they just want to think about it?

Remember this: an objection is a "yes" with a stipulation.

After all, they didn't say "no," did they? They pretty much said "not yet"or"not unless…"

In essence, an objection could be seen as a question.

Find out what the problem is and be creative. You can be accommodating without being a limp fish. Keep in mind nobody gets everything they want.

There are compromises, always. For instance, your client doesn't really expect you to find them 100% financing, with no closing costs, one day after they completed a bankruptcy. But, that won't stop them from asking for it.

It's the mark of a mortgage professional to educate the client about their particular options for their circumstances, and try to find a way to make it happen. A professional will also never shy away from telling the client "no."

After having done a few mortgages, I'm very reluctant to do another one ever again.

Why is that?

The loan officer was horrible. He changed our closing date several times, we had to come to the table with much more money than we were told originally, and the paperwork wasn't even right when we finally did get to closing. Do you want to comment on these topics?

Sure. About estimations, I always overestimate closing costs a little. I overestimate the time it will take to close and I over-quote the timeline in general. I over-gather conditions, underestimate cash-out on equity loans, and never underestimate the bank underwriter's ability to make the whole process a living hell.

The point is that I don't ever set myself up for falling short of my predictions by not having the guts to tell it like it is.

Would the realtor like getting a call saying the loan could close early? YES

Would the borrower like to find out they got an extra $1k on their cash-out? YES

Would the loan close sooner if more potential conditions were gathered to satisfy the underwriters immediately, if they asked for more supporting documentation? YES

Would it delay the closing if closing cost or the loan amount were underestimated? YES

The loan would have to go back to underwriting and all new disclosures would have to be drawn.

I also play with estimations in my own head. If I know I have a closing Friday, I'll convince myself it's Wednesday and push hard. It never fails that, when I do this, it takes all I have to close it Friday. This is a good habit to get into.

If I went to all the extra trouble to be honest and to do things the right way, because it does seem like it's tougher to do things the right way, I would want to charge accordingly. But, wouldn't I get more business if I discounted my fees?

Why would you discount your fees? Be proud of what you charge. You are a professional and deserve to earn a great living for what you do.

Would you haggle with a five-star steakhouse over their $30 steak just because you knew they only paid $8 for it, and it couldn't have taken more than about $2 in man hours to present it to you? No. They will make what they charge. If they do a good job, you'll go back and tell your friends.

You deserve whatever you charge. You set it. The clients will respect you for your honesty and integrity. Nobody would respect a discount super-center lawyer, or a drive-in loan officer, who charges just enough to keep clothes on their back. A professional needs to be in business for the long-term. To do that, a professional will charge professional fees that warrant his or her time spent helping clients the right way. I only discount fees if it's necessary, at closing, to get the deal done and if there's no other way to fix the issue.

What do you say to people when they ask what your rates are and they claim someone promised them one rate or another?

Ahhh, rate shoppers.

You know, my thinking on rate shoppers is that they're just ignorant about the process; rate is all they've been told to ask about. Maybe their dad told them to get ten offers and ask for the rates and fees. After all, that makes sense right?

Yes, it makes sense.

But, it's not the best way to find the right mortgage. It made more sense in the past, than it does today. You must educate the client once again.

In today's mortgage market, there are programs for just about anyone. The rate depends on many things: the program, income documentation, loan-to-value ratio, debt ratio, type of property, and even the time of day.

Did you know rates change sometimes twice a day?

No, I didn't.

Plus, some loan officers will trick their clients with a bait and switch technique. Rate shoppers are perfect for being lured in by this.

The loan officer will promise a low rate, which includes points, before they look at the client's details and credit, just to prevent them from shopping around.

I like to expose this to my clients and tell them that, if someone promises them a rate without properly taking a complete loan application, they're lying. It will likely end up badly for them.

Like it did for me.

Exactly. What will happen much of the time is that the deal will get just days away from closing and the loan officer will come up with some excuse about why they can't honor the rate originally promised.

Being just days away from closing on their dream home will force many clients into signing the loan docs, rather than losing the house. It's a terrible way to conduct business and has given mortgage brokers a bad name.

What is your advice to loan officers dealing with the rate question up front?

Be confident enough to tell people that neither you nor anyone else can, or should, promise them a rate without doing what is necessary to secure that funding with a lock, and only after knowing all the details of the application.

You could tell them what the rate would be in a certain situation; such as, if they have A-credit, can prove their income, have a two year stable job history, have adequate assets, and qualify for this or that particular program.

Then, you can tell them on a thirty-day lock, if locked right then, what their rate would be. My clients have to get the process started for me to give them a thorough and respectful answer. It's the only way to know I can back up what I say. After I tell them this, I take the application.

Objection overcome, client educated and not likely to shop around, armed with information against bait switchers, and they're better off just because I cared enough to have a thoughtful conversation with them.

How do you compete with those companies on TV, who offer extremely low rates and no closing costs?

Oh, you opened a can-of-worms now. There is no competition. How much business do you think a TV advertising lender gets per month?

A ton, I should think.

Also, if they provided a good service and really could offer those ridiculously low rates, with no closing costs, do you think they'd be getting referrals?

Yes, they would.

Then how fast would that company have to grow if they advertised all the time and continued to get exponential referrals?

Pretty fast.

Too fast. The truth is that they could never keep up and they'd be the largest company on the planet within a few years.

Those teaser rates are often for clients with near perfect credit, 20% down, quoted with discount points to drop the rate, and other things they disclose only in the small print at the bottom of the screen.

I doubt if anyone actually gets that rate. If I go to my best lender and see what my par rate is, and they're offering loans below that, something's fishy.

What about their claim of no closing costs?

Seriously, how can any business make money not charging anything?

It's dishonest.

Here's an example of how they do it. There are things not considered to be closing costs. Discount points and broker fees are the two I'd like to tell you about. I've seen them offer no closing costs and charge 2 discount points and a five thousand dollar broker fee. Now is that misleading or what?

Very misleading!

Also, the yield spread premium, YSP, or service release premium, SRP, is not a closing cost.

What's a YSP or SRP?

It's the difference between our negotiated wholesale buy rate and the retail rate we offer the client. The lender pays us a yield based on the difference between the two. SRP is the same thing, in essence, even though bankers will try to say it's not.

So add up the yield spread and broker fee, and use the points to counteract the impact of the yield spread, and you have yourself a profit while pulling the wool over the client's eyes. Oh, they'll leave the closing table understanding somewhat how they got the raw end of the deal. They'll tell their friends to stay away from that mortgage company.

That's why these companies have to advertise on a continuous basis to keep business coming in. It's a dishonest way of doing it and the saddest part about it is that it's no where near necessary to thrive in this business.

My clients send their friends and family to me because I was honest about the whole deal and educated them, protecting them against such blatant acts of disrespect, from the very beginning.

Their way of doing business seems to upset you. Does it make you angry?

You bet it does. It's companies like these that make our job harder, having to constantly dispel the myths that all mortgage people are crooked. They also skew the issues so that even the government regulators think we're the problem, when we're not.

That's why I do what I do, teaching constantly. I want all loan officers to know how to do things the right way.

Is there anything else you'd like to say about this?

Just this. Sometimes I listen to the radio late at night. Last night, I heard something so stupid I wanted to comment on it.

Since I'm not Jimmy Buffett I can't write a song about it. Although, sending this to him crossed my mind.

There's a mortgage company with an ad on the radio, which says something like, "if you have a $100k mortgage, and you're paying more than $200 a month you need to call us. Our payments have just been discounted...again...it sounds incredible but it's true... blah blah blah blah."

I'm not in the mortgage business and it sounds like a scam to me.

What a bunch of crap. People fall for this?

This brings me to my point.

We have a duty to educate people; all people. We have the awesome task and never ending quest to find people, who would normally fall for this, and tell them the truth about it. It's our obligation as professionals.

We no longer have the luxury of closing our fill, or whatever we feel comfortable with, and then taking a three-month vacation.

We must spread the word and do our job helping, educating, serving, and saving people from bad business ethics.

I cannot put it any more plain than that!

People's homes, families, and financial futures depend on it. If we don't help them the right way, what are the chances they'll get helped the wrong way by someone else?

The chances seem high. But, what you propose seems daunting.

It's really simple. All you have to do, besides talk to everyone who will listen, is to tell people the truth.

Tell them what you make and why you deserve to make it. Educate them. People don't really care that you make good money. They just want you to be worth it.

Great. This seems to wrap up objections, rates, fees, and your feelings about some others in your industry.

LOAN APPROVALS

Let's tone it down a little and talk about after the loan application, and after the client already wants you to help them. What if they want you to help, but they don't qualify for the loan? Did you go to a bunch of trouble for nothing?

Absolutely not. You can do a loan for everyone who wants one. Eventually.

If the client doesn't qualify for the loan program they need, put them in touch with a reputable credit restoration service. Then, all you need to do is add them on your calendar for a few months later, and keep in touch with them. You could have a pipeline of people getting credit help and calling you to get a loan afterwards. Plus, credit restoration helps people's self esteem, lowers their payments on everything they finance, and makes them really like that you took the time to help them. Everyone gets into trouble once in a while. I believe that everyone deserves a second chance.

So every loan is a "yes" eventually?

Well, now that you mention it, yes and no. Here's why it could be no:

In the mortgage business, much like in other industries, you must learn to trust your gut instinct. If the deal smells, turn it down. You'll only make your life harder by taking deals with dishonest people.

It's something to think about. It takes a long time to process a messy deal and to double check everything the client says.

What would you do with three loans like this?

Okay, now how many good clean loans could you handle if you didn't have any like this?

Five to ten, by yourself, I would imagine. You would have less stress and less time spent on them; a more rewarding experience, better morale, and you'd feel good about yourself.

Turn down, or don't even get involved with, bad business. Bad business always has a bad future.

Define bad business.

Fraudulent application information, and weird deals, with tons of hurdles for people who just aren't honest.

They're usually easy to spot because liars forget one thing. You can lie to your spouse, you can lie to your friends, you can even lie to your employer, but it's very hard to lie to your banker. We have an eye for detail and can see right through most ploys anyone could ever dream up.

We have the credit report and other documentation that paints a picture for us. If that picture doesn't match the words coming out of the client's mouth, we know something's fishy.

So, what if the deal is good but it's just complicated.

If the client has a complicated situation, or if you feel the loan application doesn't clearly explain what is going on, when you present it to a lender, write a letter to the underwriter.

At times, you must write the client's story and help put their best foot forward. It must be a true story, of course, but you can write a pitch-letter introducing the deal to a lender. Often times, it's a good idea on sub-prime loans to explain things fully.

Be willing to fight for your client if you feel they deserve financing. Illustrate why you feel the way you do, and list as many positive aspects to the loan as you can. These are called the compensating factors.

But, don't hold on like a pit bull. If you see that a lender doesn't like the deal for some reason, and rejects your rebuttal, take it to another lender. Never get ugly with a lender. You have to work in this business longer than the duration of this one deal, so keep it professional.

NUCLEUS CONCEPT

creating brochures blogging
docs processing setting closing
application
talking to clients
meetings
lunches
disclosures paperwork planning a party
business cards
printing

A FIRM FOUNDATION

It seems to me that any loan officer with enough determination and effort level could use this advice and never face a lack of business. But, with so much to consider and do, how could I possibly close a respectable number of loans by myself?

That's why I don't teach doing everything yourself. In the past, I thought it was beneficial. But, doing it by myself for a few years made me yearn for the team approach and division of duties.

You, a processor, a marketing partner, and your wholesale reps constitute a team. Even a couple of loan officers and a processor could constitute a team. Whatever the structure, it can be very rewarding. I call it the nucleus concept.

Okay, explain that to me.

Here's my illustration.

The nucleus is the center of a cell, just as a loan officer should be the center of their team. The way to start is by brainstorming. You write down every duty it takes to find clients and close loans, minus third party supporting services, like title and appraisal.

Include everything that fills your time, relating to your loan business.

Then, think about what you're good at. Ask yourself what you really love, and want, to do. Then, add these things to your primary circle. So, take a piece of paper and draw a circle. Write your favorite things in that circle.

Now, go down the list checking off those things that are absolutely necessary for you to close loans. Write the essential things, you didn't include in your circle, around the perimeter and enclose them with a bigger circle. Then, write everything else around the perimeter of the second circle. You can enclose those also, but it should look like a target with a bulls-eye and one, or two, rings. This becomes your division of duties chart.

So, now I have a chart of duties, what next?

It's simple. Just formulate your game plan to represent the chart. You personally do the things inside the nucleus. Delegate others to account for the duties listed in the second circle. Then, work on, or delegate, the things in the outside circles when you get time. Make these rainy day tasks.

What you'll find is that you'll be happier, and more productive, just doing what you love to do. You'll wake up with more passion for the day ahead.

I can see that.

Plus, by finding those who have the proper duties in their nucleus, to include those things in your second circle, you'll have a whole team that seems to fit perfectly. Find those who love to do what you don't, and are good at what you aren't.

Everyone compliments each other's strengths and weaknesses.

Exactly! If you think that way, things will come together.

We've talked about so much here it's hard to imagine any more. At this point, it seems a matter of acting on these things instead of trying to learn more things. Do you agree?

I do. It's important to implement the things you learn.

A mechanic can have thousands of tools. But, if he doesn't use them he's useless, compared to a busy mechanic with only a few tools.

JobsForLoanOfficers.com

MONTHLY TASKS

1. Send post card to your client and professional database on the 15th of each month.

2. Automatic newsletters go out to your global database every month.

3. Attend as many mortgage mixers, gatherings, or leads group lunches as you can, on a regular basis.

4. Do something relaxing every week.

   Play golf, ride horses, go fishing.

   It's important to remove yourself from the daily grind long enough to recharge your batteries.

Would you like to discuss things further, or give any more tips?

Of course. Let's see...

Keep aware of these few things to do every single month, no matter what happens in your life.

Your database should consist of 300 of your best past clients and lead sources. As you close new loans, think about the quality of your postcard database and consider culling the herd, as we say in Texas. Try to increase the quality of your database by replacing non-productive clients with more active ones, or those with higher loan amounts. It's your pick. But, keeping up the habit of increasing the quality of this particular database will increase its bang for your buck. It will increase its efficiency.

Better referrals equal better income and less work for you.

The first thing on your list should be to send out a monthly postcard. I found the U.S. post office has an online sending option where you can upload your database, create a postcard, and send with a few clicks. It's better than recruiting your family to lick envelopes. That never worked well for me.

Now remind me what to send.

What to send is up to you. I usually highlight how I helped someone recently, which let's people know how I could potentially help them.

I've done postcards to make a comment about the current market, a new product or service I have, or anything that may be enlightening or beneficial. Let them know that you're there for them just like their family doctor.

What about the automatic newsletter?

The automatic newsletter should go to everyone you can think of, who has an email address.

Everyone... Period.

There are mortgage website companies out there who can send automatic newsletters with pre-written content. I've found it to be very beneficial.

Next, you said something about mortgage mixers.

Yes. Attending meetings and mixers. There are tons of meetings going on at all times of the day on all days of the week.

There's the Realtors association, Builders association, Chamber of Commerce, Masonic and Eastern Star organizations, Rotary, Leads or Tips groups, mixers, and bank parties. Go and rub elbows. You'll have fun.

Now, finally, talking directly to the loan officers and others who may read this. What do you want to say in closing?

Just this…look, it's time for everyone to realize some truths.

It's time to realize that every sale can be, at least somewhat, an uphill battle.

Keep your head and stay calm. Things happen and all you can do is try to remain flexible and creative. Being calm will help you think of ways around the hurdles you encounter. Nobody said it was easy. It's simple, but not easy. That's why not everyone is productive and why we make so much money if we are. If you aren't productive, put yourself on a trial. Give yourself ninety days of serious hard work. I mean very hard work. Make cold calls right out of the phone book, give a card to everyone you see, hand out flyers door-to-door, and call referral sources to ask for a chance at their referrals. Do everything humanly possible, and you'll know if you have or haven't. At the end of ninety days, make a decision about changing companies, or industries, if you don't have more business than you can handle. This approach never fails. It has worked for over four hundred of my most inexperienced sales people, during good times and bad, throughout my career.

It's time to think about your future.

Think of top-notch sales people you know. Write their names down and talk to them. Ask for their advice. You can reap the benefits from their experience.

It's time to read.

Reading is one of the best ways I stay focused. I research new ideas and concepts, and I read marketing material and tailor it for my needs. Don't throw away advertising from other companies. Do you realize that company paid thousands of dollars for a marketing company, to use all the psychology they knew, to put it together? Keep it, and modify it for yourself.

It's time to be a role model.

Do things right. In a world, and profession, where so many are dishonest, do things the right way. Advertise that you do it right. Educate your clients and tell them you are of the utmost integrity and honesty. Tell them things they might not want to hear. Be different. Clients will respect that.

The key is to get working and then stay consistent. Do it every day, day after day. Don't stop for any reason, and you will succeed where others don't, all because of your persistence.

Anyone can succeed?

There is no accidental success. Those who thrive in any market, do so because of their belief in one simple truth:

In any market, at any time in history, wartime or peacetime, and with any client type, business is still being conducted. People just like you are producing business. Life doesn't stop because of some adversity, market conditions, or difficult circumstances. It just weeds out those who don't have the strength of character to go out and get it. The slower market corrects itself by this process. Less business means less fair-weather loan officers. Those who utilize all the tools at their disposal will succeed.

Now that you've had a heavy dose of realizations, it's time for action.

It's a time when all failures are past and reflection on them is therapeutic. Don't think of your failures as being bad. Without failure, there can be no success.

When I think back, I can see how all of my past experiences, even failures, contributed to my success today. Every job I've ever had taught me things I use today. Every mistake taught me something and every "chewing out" taught me to be humble. I want you to strive for excellence and success because I know it's within your grasp. You can taste reaping its rewards now.

So pump it up and reach your goals. Know the feeling you'll get when you dig in and work hard. A sense of accomplishment is a wonderful thing and I know you have the perseverance and strength to reach, even surpass, whatever your goals may be.

I urge you not to let small hurdles affect your long-term goals. There's always a way around anything and there's always something good to come out of, just about, every situation.

You must keep motivated and keep your mind sharp. Look for creative ways to market yourself.

I want you to strive for something better within yourself. Strive to do better than last month, every month. Make your career what you want it to be. The only person holding you back is you, so take advantage of this information and GO FOR IT!

I umm....wow....I need just a minute, will you excuse me?

(I notice that my ending statements have made an impact on Amelia. Maybe it's the passion with which I said them. I don't know, but my ending statements have me feeling like I just sprinted a 40-yard dash. This interview has me thinking of things I had tucked away in my mind, for years, until now.)

(She comes back in the room clearing her throat and hands me another glass of water)

Mr. Bronson...Bill.

(She walks quickly over to the ottoman of my chair and sits down. She looks excited and has a smirk on her face like a cat that just ate the canary. It makes me just a little uneasy as I wonder what's on her mind.)

I'll keep writing, of course, but I want you to take me on as an apprentice. Teach me these things in more depth. Teach me how to succeed as a loan officer.

I've always wanted to work in the mortgage business and you've made finally doing it irresistible to me. The thrill of helping a young family get into a home is something I want to experience. Just the thought of children playing in their very own yard, makes me determined to do this.

I know you're the one who can best help me, and I'll work as hard as I need to work.

Well, I can hardly resist a request and motivation like that. We will need to talk more about the particulars.

Of course. Lisa! Are you finished?

(She calls into the other room. I still feel a little strange at the moment. The feeling occurs to me that Amelia is up to something more.)

(Another woman comes in with a thick envelope about the size of loan closing paperwork and hands it to her, shooting me a quick smile.)

I want to give this to you.

(Amelia slowly hands me the envelope with quiet anticipation showing on her face.)

What is this?

It's a gift from us, well… from me, and before you open it I want to thank you for a wonderful afternoon talk. It's not often I get to speak to someone about life lessons in general, or some of the more particular things you and I discussed about the mortgage sales business.

Usually, my clients have more abstract things to tell me about the book they want to write. They don't really know how they want to present it and they don't always know what they want to include in the book.

You came here for me to write your book, but you wrote it already by dictation. I don't see that I would be able to improve on it enough to warrant my services.

You didn't need a writer. You just needed someone to ask you probing questions. I drew out of you things you had locked in your head. Plus, as a token of my appreciation for what lies ahead, I wanted to give this to you.

I had Lisa transcribe our meeting. This is what was in your head, waiting to come out. This is what you've been trying to find a way to finish. Here's your book.

(Looking down at this thick envelope, I'm speechless. I had doubted my ability to write it, and now here it is! I should have taken my own advice long ago and just done it.)

I don't know what to say. Amelia, thank you very much.

You're welcome.

Now, about being your apprentice..........................

The End

ENDING THOUGHTS

Persistence, Determination, and Faith

These three things are the main reason I have endured and excelled in the mortgage industry.

Persistence – I never give up. I don't give up on a file unless I've tried everything, I can think of, to close it. I call and ask questions, read, research, post scenarios on message boards, and call bank reps. I do everything in my power to make the most of every client situation. I never take "no" for an answer. Instead, I ask "why not?" and "who will?" I never give up on marketing. If an idea doesn't work, then so be it; I try another one. If you just can't get a client to say yes, you may be acting artificial. Try being real and just offering to help.

Determination – You must have the backbone to go after what you want. Take control of your career. You should never rely on a manager to force your nose to the grindstone. You must jump at your duties of your own free will. Get excited and stay positive. I've never seen someone with determination fail at much of anything. If you aren't being given the answers in a sippy-cup, then maybe you need to go after them. Find who knows what you don't know. Find who is excelling and ask for a moment of their time. It's your life and your career. Own it. Excel at it.

Faith – I can't say enough about faith. Without it, the game is over. Faith can work miracles, while the lack of it can cause devastation.

If you don't have faith in you ability to do your best, at least some of the time, you will never get close to your potential.

If you don't have faith that you can be a good steward of the many gifts you've been given, you will never utilize them. I don't know what your gifts are, but here are a few of mine:

1. I strive to know all I can about every important aspect of my career and life. Therefore, I have much more to offer those I intend to mentor and good advice for them, and my clients.

2. I am a philosophical kind of person. I think things out like a chess game and try to determine the best course of action for each situation. Most of the time, it's beneficial.

3. I am diplomatic and can easily talk to a wide range of people on their level.

Think of the gifts you have been given in your life and then be a faithful steward of perfecting and utilizing them. I get my strength from my faith in, and my walk with, Christ. You must find your source.

Be a real mortgage professional and help your clients to the best of your ability and creativity. You'll shine in their life as a blessing and may even get the privilege of helping their friends and family. Don't forget to ask for the business. Remember, "Determination," above?

Repeat after me, *"I will succeed in any market, at any rate, under any program, and with any underwriting department. I will excel in all that I do and will have my PDF with me at all times. Persistence, Determination, and Faith. These will help me succeed."*

Now, make a game plan and stick to it.

I look forward to hearing of your success.

Sincerely,

William B. Bronson